LET'S LOOK AT FEELINGS™

What I Look Like When I Am
·Confused·

Joanne Randolph

The Rosen Publishing Group's
PowerStart Press™
New York

Published in 2004 by The Rosen Publishing Group, Inc.
29 East 21st Street, New York, NY 10010

First Edition

Book Design: Kim Sonsky
Photo Credits: All photos by Maura B. McConnell.

Library of Congress Cataloging-in-Publication Data

Randolph, Joanne.
What I look like when I am confused / Joanne Randolph.– 1st ed.
    p. cm. – (Let's look at feelings)
Summary: Describes how different parts of a face look when a person is confused.
Includes bibliographical references and index.
ISBN 1-4042-2510-2 (library binding)
1. Human information processing in children–Juvenile literature. 2.Perception in children–
Juvenile literature. [1. Perception. 2. Miscommunication. 3. Facial expression. 4. Emotions.]
I. Title. II.Series.
BF723.I63R36 2004
152.4–dc21

                                                          2003009109

Manufactured in the United States of America

Contents

I am confused.

5

When I am confused
my eyes look up.

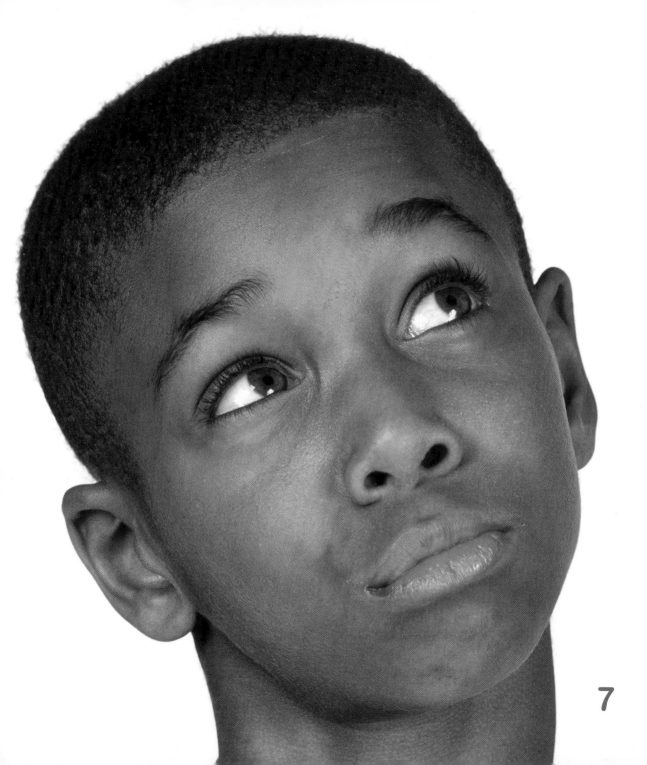

7

When I am confused my eyes look to the side.

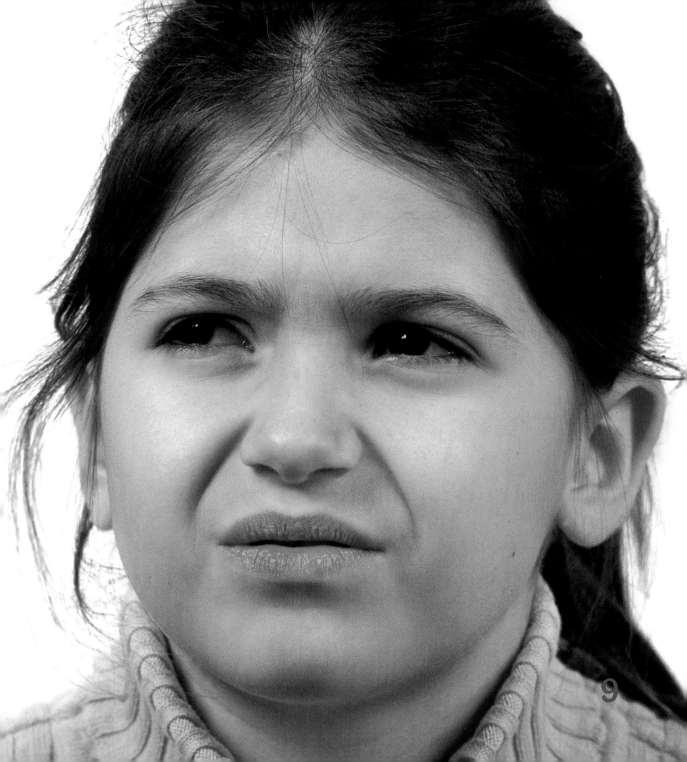
9

I get lines on my nose
when I am confused.

11

When I am confused
my cheeks get round.

13

I get lines by my mouth
when I am confused.

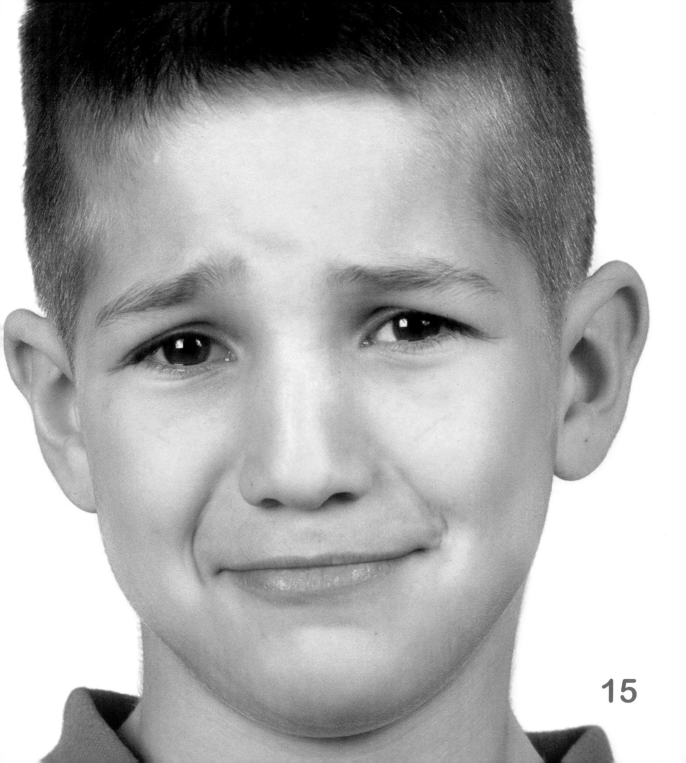

When I am confused
my mouth opens.

My mouth moves to the side when I am confused.

19

When I am confused my chin drops down.

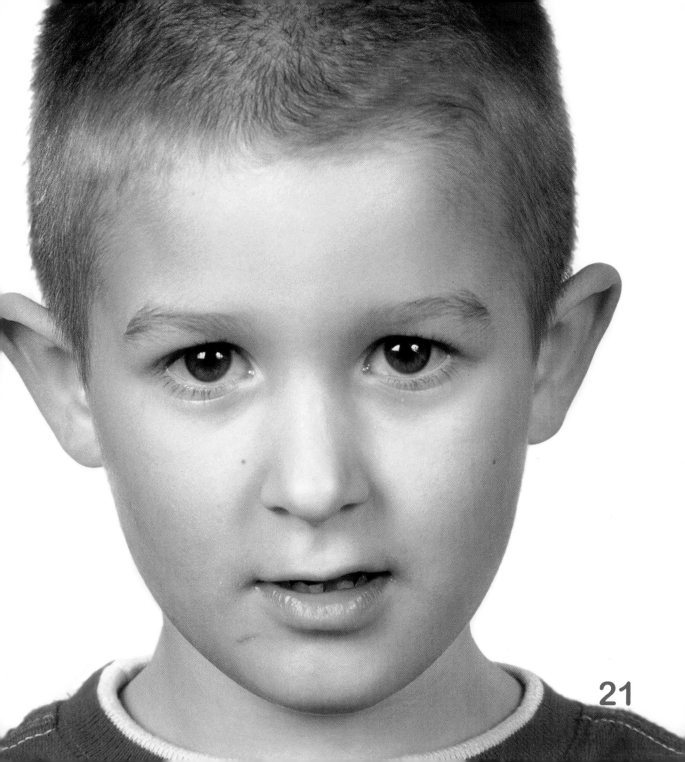

21

This is what I look like when I am confused.

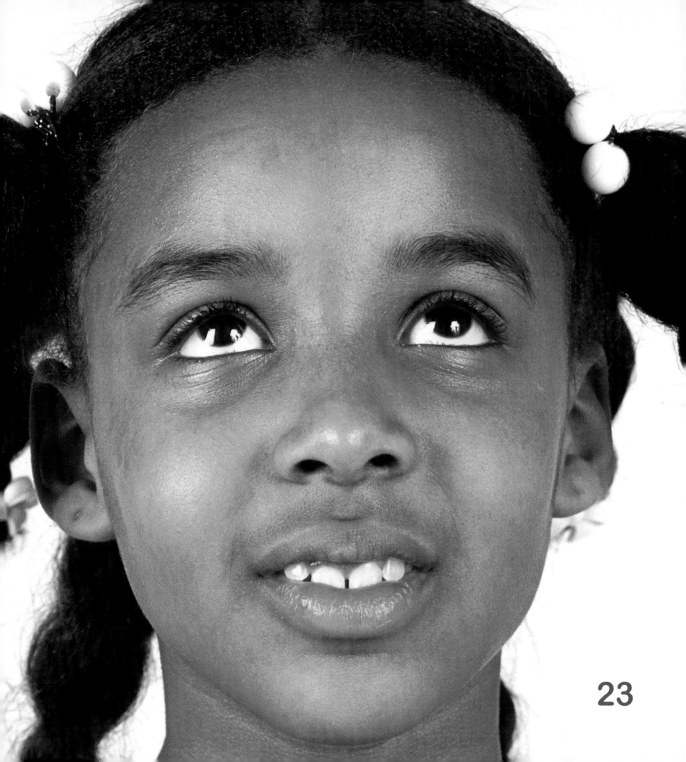

23

Words to Know

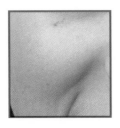

cheek

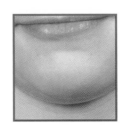

chin

eye

mouth

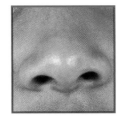

nose

Index

Web Sites

Due to the changing nature of Internet links, PowerStart Press has developed an online list of Web sites related to the subject of this book. This site is updated regularly. Please use this link to access the list:

www.powerkidslinks.com/llafe/confu/